LEAN IN

&

LET GO

A WOMEN'S GUIDE TO
CREATING A LIFE YOU LOVE

FONTELLA MOODY

LET THE WORDS CHANGE YOU

Printed in the United States of America

Acknowledgements

I want to thank my mother who has over the years showed me strength, determination and love. Thank you for introducing me to the concept of financial independence through Amway when I was a little girl and introducing me to books on tape like *Think and Grow Rich, The Magic of Thinking Big* and *The Power of Positive Thinking*. Thank you for always believing in me and telling me that I could do anything.

Thank you to my two children Elliott and Christina for allowing to me to practice being a parent with you. I love you both more than you can know and I am proud to be your mother.

Thank you to my granddaughter Chloe whose birth has changed my life and given me a greater purpose and has made it possible for me to share myself with the world in ways that surprise me.

Preface

If you feel you are in immediate danger, call the police.
If you are not currently living a life you love because of
intimate partner abuse and your relationship is violent,
seek help at your local women's shelter or call the
National Domestic Violence Hotline at 800-799-SAFE.
For information, visit their website www.thehotline.org

The purpose of this book is to inspire, motivate and
empower you to create a life of love through my personal
story of childhood molestation and experience of intimate
partner abuse. I am not giving financial, legal, psychological,
relationship or professional advice on intimate partner
abuse.

Contents

Introduction

I spent most of my life running away from anything that did not feel good, if it was outside of my comfort zone, I went the other way. I now realize that the very situation or emotion I was trying to avoid, was the very thing I needed to lean into in order to heal.

By leaning into and embracing that thing I feared and letting go of the fear, I gained my power. I also learned that the power was part of what I feared. You see as long I didn't have power, I had other people or circumstances I could blame for the problems in my life. As long as I was a victim, I did not have to take responsibility for what went wrong.

The fear may not go away, the secret is to embrace it, lean into it, take action and then let it go. I now realize, love is so much more powerful than fear.

There will always be new levels of growth, new experiences and awakenings that conjure up fear. I have discovered, that everything I wanted was just on the other side of fear. So, I act in spite of the fear, move forward in spite of the fear, and do that thing, in spite of the fear. Through leaning into my fear, taking action and letting go of the fear, I got everything I wanted: joy, peace, love and personal power.

Chapter 1

Be Clear

The convergence of becoming a grandmother and losing my grandmother put me in action to be the person I wanted to be. In my questioning and wondering whether or not my grandmother lived her life fully, I gained the courage to decide to live my life fully and to show up in the world in a way that makes a difference. In other words, I got clear about who I am, what I stand for and what I am willing to do to make it happen.

In 2013, my first granddaughter Chloe was born and I discovered a whole new meaning for being in love. There is so much joy in seeing her big smile and her bright brown eyes when she expresses herself and pretends to feed her baby dolls or change their diapers. Her birth has been the greatest gift and part of that gift was for me to decided and get clear about who I am and what I stand for. The months leading up to Chloe's birth, I developed a personal mission statement which is simply to thrive. I thought about what I wanted for her and for my children Christina and Elliott, or Ekay as Elliot likes to be called. Then I realized that my desire to thrive expanded to every person in my life: my family, friends, employees, customers and people I hadn't even met yet. I desire for everyone in my world to reach their full potential and if I can play a positive role in helping them get there, then I am even happier.

December of 2014, my grandmother who had a stroke ten years prior began to decline in health and in January I traveled to see her for what would be my final good bye to her. She passed away the following month. My grandmother was my "Mama" and I loved her dearly. I was lucky to have her as my only sitter until I was thirteen years old, and I am so grateful for her love and demonstration of grace.

Experiencing the birth of my granddaughter and the transition of my grandmother and the incredible love I have for them both, I began to realize the years that my grandmother deferred her happiness, joy and self-expression. I wondered what her life would have been like if she lived it fully during my childhood. I wondered the impact she could have made if she lived her life without fear and gave herself fully to the world.

Deciding who I desired to be, required me to clear away the clutter: physically and mentally I needed to clear away pieces I no longer needed or wanted. The Renaissance artist Michelangelo said about his masterpiece David when he was asked about the difficulty of creation, "It is easy. You just chip away the stone that doesn't look like David". In seeking clarity, I needed to peel away the pieces that did not represent me so I could discover what was hidden beneath.

Have you ever looked around at your surroundings and everything seemed clean, but when you looked closer, dug a litter deeper, you found clutter? Maybe the kitchen appeared clean because the clutter was tucked away in the kitchen drawer that has: old mail, broken utensils, a lighter that doesn't work and a collection of stuff you were afraid to throw away. Maybe your bedroom looks clean and organized, but when you open your closet or look under the bed, there are dresses that don't fit and a clutter of shoes gathering dust. Well, just like you have clutter tucked away out of sight in your home, you have clutter or confusion going on in your mind. If you pay attention, you will see how it shows up in your life and in your relationships. The following strategies will assist you in gaining clarity.

Be Clear In Your Thinking

Get clear about what you truly believe is true for you and look for contradictions. Contradictions cause a loss of power, struggle and a lack of forward movement. A contradiction is when you say I want to be wealthy and you also say money is evil or it is when you say you want to be married and you also say, men / women are no good. These thoughts are confusion and contradictions and until you clear away the beliefs that do not support your true desires, what you want will not show up or if it does, you will push it away. So get clear about what you are creating for yourself first in your mind and let go of the thoughts that do not support your vision.

Be Clear With Your Words

I discovered Dr. Wayne Dyer in the early part of the new millennium and loved his teachings on daily affirmations. An affirmation is a positive statement that starts out with "I am." Our language is powerful and when we clearly articulate who we are, what we are doing and how we are being, we create just that. For years, I said I wanted to write a book, but it did not actually start to happen until I said, "I am going to write a book." Do you see the difference between, "I want to write a book," and "I am writing a book"? I want to be happy verses I am happy. Wanting to be happy creates a longing to be happy, not happiness. I am happy creates being happy and I get to be happy right now because I said so, and the best part is in spite of circumstances, I get to decide to be happy.

If going from depressed right to, "I am happy" is too much of leap for you, try one of my favorite affirmations:

"Every day in every way I am getting better."

No matter how good life is this one works and lines up with my life's mission to thrive which is all about getting better.

Clear the Physical Clutter

Before you get started on creating your ideal life, let's first clear away the clutter. Look at your home, your office, your car or anywhere else you can physically see clutter. Start small; pick an area you can clean out today. It can be as simple as choosing to de-clutter the top drawer of your night stand or the glove box in your car. The goal here is just to get started. If you find one sock that you have been waiting for the mate to magically appear, throw it away. If you find a pair of shoes you have not worn in three years, donate them. The point is to clear away as much clutter as you can and releasing items that you do not need or use any more is a great way to get going.

Now that you are in action, keep going! Look for the next area to clear away and release more of your old, unused clutter. As you clean, de-clutter and organize pay attention to how your feel. Are you noticing yourself getting anxious about throwing away old stuff or are you starting to get energized by the progress you have made? Whatever is coming up for you is good, just pay attention. If you find yourself having trouble getting started, call on a friend. Tell them your plan to de-clutter and ask for their help by having them ask you how it is going.

List six or more things you discovered about yourself as you cleaned and organized your space?

_____

_____

_____

_____

_____

_____

_____

_____

Clear the Mental Clutter

Now let's de-clutter the confusion and contradictions you have in your head. Let's take a look at what's going on in there and identify some thoughts that are working against you.

On the left hand side write down what you want to create for yourself and then on the right hand side write the first contradicting thought that pops in your head. Take note of who told you the contradicting thought, does it make sense and is it serving you to get you what you want?

I am going to....   But......

I am going to buy a house   *But, owning a house is debt*

_____   _____

_____   _____

_____   _____

_____   _____

_____   _____

_____   _____

_____   _____

_____   _____

Let Go and Lean into the Goal

Imagine that you can have anything you want, the world is perfectly aligned and you will receive or accomplish every desire you imagine. You have now identified the contradictions. What are you committed to doing to release the contradictions to achieve your goals? What will say to yourself when the contradicting thoughts come back to you?

On the left hand side write down what you want to create for yourself and then on the right hand side write down the largest benefit of achieving your goal.

I am going to....   And......

I am going to buy a house   *And, I will earn equity*

_____   _____

_____   _____

_____   _____

_____   _____

_____   _____

_____   _____

_____   _____

_____   _____

What Could Your Life Be Like?

Now using the same concept let's create your ideal prefect life; where would you live, with whom are you living, what are you doing for a living, how much money are you making a year and how are you taking care of yourself? Write your answers down in the present tense as if you already have what you want.

I....   And......

I live near the beach   *And, I love the sun & water*

_____   _____

_____   _____

_____   _____

_____   _____

_____   _____

_____   _____

_____   _____

_____   _____

Putting It All Together

Now that you have created your list of what you are going to be, do and have, let's review it and get to the core of what you really want.

The real question is why do you want what you want? In the answer to that question, you will find your real goal. Do you want to advance in your career, so that you will be successful? Do you want to improve your relationships so that you will be happy? Do you want to start a business so that you will be free from a boss?

Examples

Thing to Have or Do	*Ways of Being*
Buy a house	Grounded or Settled
Get married	Loveable
Travel the world	Adventurous
Start a business	Free
Graduate College	Accomplished
Have a baby	Joyful

More "Ways of Being"

Loving	Joyful	Empowered
Free	Appreciative	Enthusiastic
Happy	Optimistic	Hopeful
Content	Sexy	Attractive
Generous	Successful	Grateful
Powerful	Peaceful	Fun
Focused	Passionate	Positive
Accepting	Blessed	Beautiful

Take some time to get clear about what you truly desire to do and what you desire to have, and how you will be when you reach your goal.

I will have or do   So, will I be

_____   _____

_____   _____

_____   _____

_____   _____

_____   _____

_____   _____

_____   _____

_____   _____

_____   _____

_____   _____

_____   _____

_____   _____

_____   _____

In addition to creating with your "I am" statement, the other secret to getting what you want is in "being" however you think you will be when you reach your goal or be however you think you need to be in order to reach your goal. The beauty is you get to decide in this very moment how you will be. If you think that getting a promotion at work will make you powerful, be powerful. If you think that losing twenty pounds will make you sexy, be sexy. If you think that being adventurous is what it takes to book your first cruise, then be adventurous. Be what you want to be right now. You can have, do and be whatever you get clear about; focus your attention to; articulate in words and put into action.

Chapter 2

Be Courageous

"I learned that courage was not the absence of fear, but the triumph over it. The brave man is not he who does not feel afraid, but he who conquers that fear." —Nelson Mandela

You might find in your quest to create a life you love, that old emotional clutter is getting in the way and sometimes cleaning that up takes courage. At the lowest point in my life I wanted to be happy and that required me to be courageous. My greatest fear was to be exposed, for people to know the secrets I harbored from my childhood.

My best friend (I will call Jennifer) lived two doors from me. I thought Jennifer had the perfect family and life, her parents were married; they went to church every Sunday and her mother bought her pretty church dresses from a department store. In my eight-year-old mind she had it all.

I loved to play at Jennifer's house because she had a basement with a play area where we would play house, pretend to cook and to take care of our babies. My doll was a Baby Crissy and she had a black pony tail that grew. I would pull her hair to make it grow long and then pull the long white string in her back to make it short again. I had a wardrobe of clothes for her and treated her just like a real baby, pretending to feed her, bath her and change her diaper. Jennifer would "babysit" for me if I had to go to work or to the store. We had a ball!

On weekends, I would stay the night at Jennifer's house and on Sundays I would go to church with her family. I learned that we had to give money in Sunday school and her parents made sure we each had a quarter to put in the offering plate. I really wanted to keep my quarter to buy watermelon Now & Later candy or Red Vine licorice. One Sunday, after putting my quarter in the offering, I found a quarter while I was playing outside. To me that was a sign from God, that as long I did what I was supposed to do, He would take care of me.

Jennifer was living the life I longed for, a mother and a father, a sister and a brother, church on Sunday and family traditions. I was an only child and my grandparents had divorced by the time I was born. After their divorce, my grandfather moved to another state and that left my grandmother with six kids still at home. My parents had never married and my father was not a part of my life. As much as I loved going to church with Jennifer's family, I felt ashamed that my parents were not married. Although I knew my father, I really did not have a father. He lived not far from us, but I did not spend time with him or call him. My mother made an effort to connect us by taking me to his house, but that only caused me make comparisons of what he had verses what we had. I looked around at his house and at his cars and came to the conclusion that he should be doing more for me. I was not only ashamed, but also angry.

My father had nine kids by seven different women; therefore, my best friend Jennifer's family seemed perfect in comparison to mine. It's odd how my joy of going to church with her was over shadowed by the fear of sin and judgment or at least my feelings of being judged. I really wanted my mother to come to church. I didn't just want her to come to church; I wanted her to be one those church ladies. I wanted it all, the mom, the dad, the sister and the family traditions. Instead, I was an eight year-old only child who spent way too much time alone.

Jennifer had an older sister and an older brother who lived with her. When I went to her house we mostly played with our dolls off to ourselves. One of the Saturday nights that I slept over, her brother let us play in his room and watch TV. I am not sure how old he was, but I am sure he was in high school. He loved Kong Fu and he liked to practice using his Nun Chucks and doing his Bruce Lee kicks over our heads.

That night, as we watched TV with him while lying on his bed, he showed us his penis. I remember being shocked that it was so big, I had only seen the penises of baby boys and had no idea that they grew to be so big. He put it next to my forearm and it was the same size as my arm. He told me take off my panties and I told him no and pulled away. Jennifer said, "It's ok we do this all the time." He explained that he was going to put his penis in me. Now that seemed impossible to me and there was no way that was going to work. I continued to tell him no, but he got on top of me and tried entering me. Just like I thought, it did not work.

I started screaming and pushing him off of me. It hurt, and I wanted to get away from him. I was crying and trying to get away, and he started telling me to be quiet and told me not to tell anyone what he had done. He promised that he would buy my anything I wanted as long as I didn't tell. I made Jennifer lay next to him, and I curled up against the wall. My model ideal family had just hurt me in ways my natural family had never done.

That next week, I obsessed over the things I expected him to buy me for keeping silent. I kept asking him when he would get me my dollhouse, that's what I wanted: a dollhouse, a doll stroller and a dream kitchen. I had it all planned out. I would get everything I ever wanted in exchange for my silence. The problem was I was scared of what he would do to me and worried about my mom finding out and what she would do to me. I was also ashamed of what God would think. I started wetting the bed and was embarrassed that I was wetting the bed. I would go to sleep hoping that I could make it through the night, but in the morning there would be a yellow wet spot where I slept.

When I was twelve, we moved and I lost touch with Jennifer and her family and I tucked away my memory of her and her brother, but it was always lurking right under the surface. Lurking with those feelings of not being good enough because I came from a single parent family and the feelings of shame, blame and guilt.

In junior high school I met all new friends, one of the first was Tracy. She was smart, talked a lot and loved having fun. Over the years Tracy become my confidant, therapist, cheerleader and the sister I always wanted. She was also one of the first people I told about being molested and just having her to talk to helped to relieve some of the suffering I was hiding.

I did not have the courage to tell my mother about Jennifer's brother until my mid-thirties and even then I did tell her everything. Through sobbing tears, still ashamed and full of guilt and blaming both my mother and father for my pain, I shared the story. If my father had done his job and been there to protect me, it would not have happened. If my mother was paying more attention, she would have seen that it wasn't safe for me to spend so much time with that family. If I had just fought back more, it would have not happened. It was everybody's fault!

Before I talked to my mother I shared my story with a counselor who encouraged me to tell her. I had a lot of fear and anxiety that had built up over the years and just the thought of telling her would make me overwhelming nervous.

By finally telling my mother, I learned I had the courage to do the thing that scared me the most. I also realized that I was living with shame, blame and guilt because I did not understand that my decision to stay silent was born from a child's mind who could not conceive of the secrets weight. Having that talk with my mother brought me one step closer to my own freedom and the ability to grow up my inner child, for the grown up me to make the decision to find my voice and to step into my power.

Look in your own life and see if there is an area you are holding on to negative emotions because you have consciously or unconsciously decided to avoid the issue or situation that caused it. Who is a safe person you can talk to: your pastor, priest or spiritual advisor, your best friend, a counselor, or your spouse?

What are you avoiding - an event or a feeling?

_____
_____
_____
_____

What are you afraid will happen if you face what you are avoiding?

_____
_____
_____
_____

Who is a safe person you can talk to?

_____
_____
_____
_____

When will you talk to them?

_____
_____
_____

What surprised you about having the conversation?

_____
_____
_____
_____

Chapter 3

Be In Action

There are ways of being that will help move you closer to creating a life you love: resourceful, courageous, responsible, determined and focused, but most importantly you must be in action. Creating a vision board as a tool to help visualize your ideal life will keep in front of you your desires and help to answer- the now what? There was a popular movie and book that inspired people to create vision boards as a way to stay focused and manifest their desires. One of the biggest misconceptions I have found in hosting vision board parties is all you have to do is create the board, look at it every day and pray. Yes, I know pray does change things, but there is also the saying, "take one step and He will take two". You have to take the first step and get in action.

The more actions you take, the more actions you will become excited to take. Things just start to unfold; circumstances start to point you in the right direction, and people show up who have the answers or help you need. If you are extremely logical and analytical, you can create a formal action plan and then execute that plan. If you are more of a free spirit and want to let your intuition guide you, go for it. Your approach really does not matter, as long as you get into action.

In 2006 because of a company restructure, I left an eighteen year career in retail. Not only did I change companies, I changed industries moving into insurance and financial services. I left a full-time job with steady paychecks and great benefits to pursue my dream of being a business owner. This has been the scariest and most rewarding decisions of my life.

To start over mid-career in an industry that I did not know, a business I had no clue how to run and to be self-employed for the first time, I needed vision, constant action and my Faith. I knew the only option for me was success and my big vision was for the second half of my life to be greater than the first half and I wanted my business to thrive. I took every step that made sense for me to take. I went back to college and got my bachelor's degree in Management Studies. I joined industry associations and volunteered in leadership roles in order to learn more about the business. I joined the Chamber of Commerce and other business networking groups to surround myself with other business owners. I attend industry workshop, business workshops, marketing workshops and sales seminars. If there was a course, a workshop, a webinar or coaching program, I did it.

Ten years later and I have a thriving business, with loyal employees, a life-style beyond what I imagined and a career I love because I dared to be courageous and to be creative by creating a vision board.

Visualize your Life

Let your creative juices flow as you start to design your ideal prefect life. One of the ways I do this is through vision boards. A vision board is a place to capture all of your dreams and inspirational images to help you visualize the life you are creating. The purpose of the board is to keep you focused on what is important to you and what you focus on expands. The fun of creating the board is in doing the research before you start putting the board together. Look on line or in magazines to get an idea of all the things you love. At first you might focus on fashion, your home, your car or your overall image. Your focus can be on money, your spirituality or faith, your relationships, your career, your health or any other area of your life that is important to you. Make sure to capture your way of being: happy, confident, loving, powerful or joyful. Look for images that represent the life you are leaning into.

Do you want to run a marathon, be a body builder or travel the globe? Find pictures of people doing exactly what you want to do and include everything. If you are looking for inspiration, tap into your social media circles. These are average everyday people just like you and I am sure you will find someone living an extraordinary life. Someone you know has already climbed Mount Everest, traveled to Fiji, bought their first house, got married, had a baby and landed their dream job, and so can you!

How to create your vision board

Before you get started, gather all of your supplies for the board.

- Your favorite board: cork board, poster board, foam-core board or magnetic board
- Scissors, tape, push-pins, glue or magnets
- Fun stickers, decals, colored paper, or post-it notes
- Markers, crayons, or pens
- Family & personal photos
- Magazines or printed images form the internet
- Your favorite affirmations or "I am" statements

There are no rules in creating the board, so be as creative as you like. Include your affirmations, images of how you will feel and what you want. If you are a techie and prefer to create your vision board on line using your phone or tablet, here are few of my favorite apps that have great images and easy to navigate vision board building menus, just search the APP Store or Google Play:

- Success Vision Board by Jack Canfield
- Vision Board by Astroport
- Happy Tapper Vision Board
- Bloom
- Corkulous Pro
- DreamCloud
- VisuaLife

"The more we see ourselves as a vibrant, successful, inspiring person who boldly declares and manifests her vision, the more we become just that." — Kristi Bowman

When you look back over your vision board and your list of desires, what is missing? What was the one thing you weren't bold enough to include in your vision? What goal seemed too big, too audacious and too scary to go for? That is the thing you probably need to add to your list; consider putting it on your vision board and start working towards it.

As soon as you do this, all of your doubts and fears will show up. The voice of your mother, your father or some other person with good intentions to protect you will show up and remind you why you cannot do it or shouldn't do it. For me it was and still is the voice of my favorite aunt. She is just a few years older than me, and we grew up together. When we were kids, if I ever talked about doing anything, her favorite response was, "Who do you think you are?" Today she would never say that to me. Her response was that of child being a child, and I use it as motivation when I set my goals high. Hearing her say: "Who do you think you are?" pushes me to be my bold self.

You might be faced with the same challenge, and I am encouraging you to be bold enough to keep moving forward to know when it is really you and when it is really the fears of your friends or family that are playing a tape in your head.

Use your vision board to place positive and bold affirmations that show the world who you are and to remind yourself in case someone asks you: "Who do you think you are?" Possible answers you can use:

- 🌿 I am bold
- 🌿 I am beautiful
- 🌿 I am courageous
- 🌿 I am smart
- 🌿 I am sassy

Now you take it from here and list out your own.

I am _____

I am _____

I am _____

I am _____

I am _____

I am _____

Getting Into Action

What are three logical action steps for you to take in order to reach your most important goal?

_____

_____

_____

_____

_____

_____

When will you complete your action steps?

_____

_____

_____

_____

_____

_____

Chapter 4

Be Consistent

"It's not what we do once in a while that shapes our lives. It's what we do consistently." — Anthony Robbins

Stop changing your mind! You got clear about the life you are creating, you created your vision board, you cleared away some emotional clutter, and you have taken action to create your dream life. Well, if you are like me, you might have run into some road blocks. Things on the surface don't look like they are working out in your favor. You want to retreat. Don't!

Do not change your mind and revert back to your old life or your old way of being. Stay consistent and stay committed to your vision. See it through until that experience, thing or way of being is realized. Keep going!

I met my first husband when I moved to the Washington DC area in 1989. He made me laugh and kept life fun, but after having my daughter and getting married, we started fighting more than having fun. As my career progressed and his didn't he become controlling and started having extra marital affairs. Every fight was the same, I wanted a divorce and he would say, "You can go, but you will never take my kids". The threat of losing my kids seemed real, so I would always retreat, we would make up and things would be calm for a few weeks.

Then one Friday night in 1999 my husband came home late, and the kids and I were already a sleep. We had been arguing for weeks, so I was sleeping in our guestroom. I woke up to him picking up the bed and throwing it against the wall with me it. He wanted to know why I did not come straight home from work, where I was before he went out. I ran out of the room, telling him to just leave and as usual he said he would only leave with our kids. I stood up to him and told him that he wasn't taking our kids anywhere, but I want him to leave.

He grabbed me by my neck, threw me on the floor with his hands still around my neck, straddled me at my waist and leaned over me to put pressure on my neck. I could not breath, all I could do is kick my legs and grab his hands as I wondered how long it takes to die. I thought that day would my last day. Then just as unexpectedly as he grabbed me, he got up and started packing a bag- like nothing happened. I ran into the hallway and pushed all the panic buttons on our alarm system for the police, fire department and ambulance. Hitting the panic buttons set off sirens in the house, and he ran before the police arrived.

I had seen him throw furniture, lock me in the car, over talk me and other signs of aggression, but never had he actually physically attached me. Finally, I had enough and I was scared enough to involve the court system and to get a restraining order. Funny thing about restraining orders, yes they are intended to protect victims, but they also aggravate perpetrators of intimate partner abuse. Once he realized he was losing control over me, my husband became more threatening and even though he was out of the house I was actually more afraid than before.

I wanted out, I wanted peace of mind and I wanted to be happy again and knew if I gave in and went back to him, I would not have the life that I wanted. I kept moving forward and filed for a divorce, through sleepless nights and panic filled days, I pressed on. Eventually the threats and calls stopped as he had to piece together his own life, where was he going to live, how was he going to parent and what was he going to do to move forward?

It wasn't easy, but the following year we were divorced and I could finally start to see the life I imagined for myself starting to come together. So decided ahead of time to commit to your goals and no matter how difficult it gets, stay determined and do not give up.

Chapter 5

Be Authentic

"To share your weakness is to make yourself vulnerable; to make yourself vulnerable is to show your strength."

— Criss Jami

In the late nineties, I was a huge fan of Iyanla Vanzant and I listened to her books on tape during my one hour commute to and from work. One of her favorite sayings was, "tell the truth and shame the devil" and I have come to understand just how powerful being honest can be. I mean honest in all areas of my life, in all relationships in my life and with myself.

My truth is after I was molested by Jennifer's brother, I began to eat. I had a lot of alone time and a lot of unsupervised time. I would take change out of my mother's purse and sneak off to the Stop & Go, the local convenience store and I would buy penny candy and pepperoni sticks. I would skip back home and eat up all the candy before I got there, so my mother would never know.

Over the years, I still ate candy, then it was sun flower seeds, then it was gnawing off my fingernails. I stopped biting my nails in college, so it was back to eating food again. In college I gained the freshman fifteen and binged on Domino's Pizza and Jamaican Almond Fudge ice cream. I didn't equate my weight gain to binge eating and thought I was just big-boned. After all that's what people used to say when I was kid. I was always a little chunky or at least I thought I was and eating tons of candy as a kid had to have put some extra pounds on me. I was always a little bigger than my mother and that didn't make sense. I thought I must have had some type of metabolism problem, and connecting the dots to over eating never occurred to me.

If I felt stressed I wanted to eat. If I was bored, I wanted to eat. If I was anxious, I wanted to eat. I just wanted to eat. At first I just wanted large portions, then I wanted seconds and thirds of meals. It was like I could not get full. I was not always like this, I used to cry if my mother tried to make me eat when I wasn't hungry. What happened? Now I could eat at the drop of a hat. What was different? What was the turning point?

Forty years later, for the first time, I remembered the meal Jennifer and I had the morning after the incident with her brother; eggs and bacon on whole wheat toast with red Kool Aid. I remembered sitting up late that night eating Ritz crackers and Cheez Whiz with Jennifer in her basement. That memory came to me when I forty-six. Finally I could connect the dots back to that period in my life when I was overwhelmed with fear, guilt and shame and I was only eight year old.

I am still not sure that knowing the cause makes it any easier, but it sure does take away the mystery and it gives me permission to go easy on myself, I was only eight for God's sake. Now here is the challenge, can my fifty-year-old self take charge of the eight-year-old who is running the show when it come to my health and fitness?

Of course I can! I am safe now, there is no threat and no one to blame. The only one responsible for my health is me, so it time to let it go and lean into the healthy life I deserve.

Do not mistake being honest with being cruel, angry or bitter in your communication with people. You do not get a free pass to be cruel and freely give your opinion of people, their choices, or their actions. Your truth has nothing to do with your opinion, it has to do with you and what is going on with you. Being honest simply means you state your truth in the most loving and respectful way.

What have you been hiding from yourself and the world?

_____

_____

_____

_____

_____

_____

_____

_____

"The privilege of a lifetime is to become who you truly are."
— C.G. Jung

I was blessed to be exposed to books on positive thinking like *Think and Grow Rich, The Magic of Thinking Big* and *The Power of Positive Thinking* at an early age. When I was in elementary school my mother sold Amway and I got to go with her to her meetings and hear the motivational stories about people who worked hard and were successful. Those books and my belief in God and His ability to change any situation gave me an unwavering faith that everything would work out in my favor. That same faith and positive thinking, other people saw as a weakness is what helped me through the challenges in my life.

Well, guess what? My Faith and my positive outlook on life is part of who I am and I love it! When I was younger, I would allow other people's opinions about my personality to create doubt in myself, but now I know it is part of what makes me uniquely me. I love all the parts of me: my strengths and my weaknesses. I embrace what I do well and give myself permission not to be good at everything and to ask for the help on the things I do not do well. Praise God, I do not have to be perfect and neither do you! Just be you.

What about you do you just love?

_____

_____

_____

_____

_____

What about do wish were different?

_____

_____

_____

_____

_____

What is good about the parts you wish were different?

_____

_____

_____

_____

_____

How are you uniquely you in both the parts you love and parts you wish were different?

_____

_____

_____

_____

_____

How is the world blessed to have you in all that you are?

_____

_____

_____

_____

_____

Chapter 6

Be Transparent

"Don't ever let anyone put out your light because they are blinded by it." — *Shannon L. Alder*

When I was in elementary school I remember attending vacation bible school and singing, "This Little Light of Mine". That song made me so happy even though I did not understand the meaning behind it, I just knew it felt good. Well today that song still make me happy and I get excited about sharing my gifts and now have a new felt purpose in sharing. The best part is because they are gifts, we do not have to try to make anything happen, we just get to be who we are and let who you are shine through. Don't be stingy in sharing yourself or your gifts and watch the world reward you.

What do you love to do?

_____

_____

_____

_____

_____

_____

What do you know you are good at?

_____
_____
_____
_____
_____
_____

What do other people tell you you are good at?

_____
_____
_____
_____
_____
_____

What is the gift you are being stingy with?

_____
_____
_____
_____
_____
_____

How would the world be impacted if you shared your gift?

_____

_____

_____

_____

_____

_____

What is the one thing you can do to let your light shine?

_____

_____

_____

_____

_____

Chapter 7

Be Powerful

"The most common way people give up their power is by thinking they don't have any." — Alice Walker

Have you ever had something have such a strong hold you that you lost all your power and self-expression? For me it happened while I was in college at the University of Washington the summer between my sophomore and junior year. I earned an internship at IBM requiring me to travel from Washington State to Poughkeepsie, New York. I was so excited, I felt like a world traveler.

The air was fresh and clean and the landscape was beautiful with rows of trees and manicured grass at Vassar College, my new home for the summer. My dorm room was small, but just big enough for a twin sized bed, a dresser, a desk and a chair. That first week at IBM and Vassar I quickly made new friends connecting with a tall dark junior from the Bronx, Marty and a quirky light skinned junior from Georgia Tech, Keith.

About half way through our internship Marty, Keith and I decided to drive down to Washington DC for a weekend trip. We all packed into Keith's red Ford Mustang and hit the road, blasting reggae music and singing at the top of our lungs for most of the trip. I would stay with my uncle and his family for the weekend and Marty and Keith would pick me up on Sunday for the trip back to New York. I remember being so excited to see my favorite uncle; I admired him from a far. He was my standard for what I thought the perfect husband, father and son should be. He was well educated, he had a great job, his wife was beautiful and he sent money home to his mother (my grandmother) every year. If we had a problem back in Washington State, we called on him.

That weekend my entire emotional life crumbled as the uncle I respected cupped my breast in his hand and confessed his attraction to me. Shirtless with gray hairs on his chest and a receding hair line he looked like he was 80 years old to me, although I am sure he was in his forties. Chills ran down my back and I felt like I was going to be sick, then my heart sank into stomach and I was paralyzed as the tears ran down my face, flowing like water from a faucet. He kissed me in my mouth, and I pulled away sobbing. He went on to tell me, "I have been attracted to you since you were 15." He then thanked me for not "going off" on him and making him feel bad. I couldn't believe it. Here he is thanking me, and I can barely move; I cannot think straight; I cannot function, and I am in shock. I remember thinking, "Not you too?"

Sunday afternoon as planned Marty and Keith picked me up and we begin our drive back to New York. I was in the front passenger seat as they began to share their stories about the weekend. The air for me was thick, and I felt heavy as it was clearly my turn to share. I curled into a ball, hugging my knees and broke into tears. I sobbed the entire ride back to Vassar and did not share my story with the boys. It must have been 11:00 pm when we rolled back onto campus and unpacked the car under the parking lot street lamps. Simply saying good night I retreated to my dorm room and immediately called my mother and aunts back in Washington State.

Devastated, angry and full of regret that I did not pick up a lamp or some other blunt object and bash in his head, one by one I share my story with my family. One by one, they don't believe me. One by one they tell me to keep quiet. One by one, they crush me. All I can think is I do not matter, no one cares about me, protect him and his family, that's what's important. So, again I stuffed my feelings away, just like I did when I eight years old.

At the end of the summer, I returned to the University of Washington and resumed my engineering studies. As I moved through my day, I was now trying to cover up the feelings of shame, embarrassment, worthlessness, hurt and anger. It was too much for me to handle; I would start crying in class and slowly isolated myself from both my friends and my family. I was depressed.

One day I woke up and decided to throw away every text book and I withdrew from my classes. The following week I applied to Western Washington University and changed my major to fashion merchandising. It felt safe, I left an environment dominated by men and was now in classes with all female students and teachers.

The fashion industry was a safe haven for me and allowed me to avoid dealing with all the negative emotions and tuck away my encounter with my uncle. It was so safe, I stayed there for eighteen years.

Over the years, I kept telling my mother and aunts about the impact my uncle's actions had on me and finally my mother believed me. My oldest aunt however did not and her advice was, "stuff like this happens in families, you get over it". The reality was I wasn't getting over it and I was living a lie still attending family functions and he was there and I was pretending I was ok. I had given up my power by pretending I was ok when I really wasn't. I had given up my power by making him and his family more important than me and my well-being.

I decided to stop being quiet and to tell his family and my family not out of anger for him but out of love for me. I was demanding that they pay attention to me and how I felt. I deserved to be free of his secret and it was my responsibility to make that happen. So I took responsibility for my happiness and discovered my power.

Where have you not taken responsibility in your life?

_____
_____
_____
_____
_____
_____

Where have you been a victim?

_____

_____

_____

_____

_____

_____

What was your part in the outcome?

_____

_____

_____

_____

_____

_____

How will you take responsibility and step into your power?

_____

_____

_____

_____

_____

_____

Chapter 8

Be Free

"Some of us think holding on makes us strong; but sometimes it is letting go." —Hermann Hesse

I always had this obsessive curiosity about how my life developed and love to analyze how my personality and belief system developed. There is a cause and effect from the trauma I experienced, but I didn't see it as trauma and I would have told you that I was "fine". I saw it as a secret that I tucked away, but the problem was, it wasn't tucked completely away. It became emotion clutter that come out by me being cold, defensive, angry and depressed.

Life for me became overwhelming after my divorce and now being a single parent myself, I was completely stressed working and raising two children. I started looking for answers first going to counseling, then bible study, women's conferences, reading self-help books, seminars and then coaching. You name it, and I probably tried it in my quest to be happy.

One of the most consistent messages I received was to forgive. Oh, it sounds so easy, but it has taken me a life-time to forgive myself and the people in my life who I thought hurt me in some way. It was so much easier to be angry, to have someone to blame and to make other people the villain in my life-story. Years went by and me forgiving my uncle, just was not happening, until one day I realized I was angry at my entire family! Angry because I wanted someone to acknowledge my hurt and care enough to stand up for me. When I could finally get in touch with my true feelings, I was able to release my anger and I was able to forgive them all.

I forgave my parents, my best friend's brother, my husbands, my aunts and my uncle. I now see how freeing it is to let go of the anger, shame, guilt and blame, through the act of forgiveness. It clears the way to make room for your power to emerge. Decide to forgive. Forgiveness, blesses you with peace.

Forgive Anyone Who Hurt You

Who are you blaming for causing you hurt, shame or guilt?

_____

_____

_____

_____

_____

Forgive Yourself

What are you blaming yourself for that is causing you hurt, shame or guilt?

_____

_____

_____

_____

_____

Forgive and Let Go of the Pain

Write a letter to each person who hurt you, including yourself expressing your gratitude for their actions and how they have helped to shape who you are. What did they allow you to learn about yourself? Express your forgiveness for their action. Read the letter to yourself ten times and then burn it. Do not mail the letter.

Chapter 9

Be Grateful

"Acknowledging the good that you already have in your life is the foundation for all abundance." — Eckhart Tolle,

A funny thing happens when you start being grateful and showing gratitude, your complaints starts to magically disappear. In my need to find blame for what I thought was wrong with my childhood I naturally blamed my parents. I think this is the natural path from childhood to adulthood. When I look back at my life and my parent's life, now I see their love and their fears. I see a single mother who worked hard during the day and took college courses at night to get her associates degree. I see a mother who intentionally moved us to the suburbs, so I could attend better schools. I see a mother who put her life on hold and moved from Atlanta to Maryland to help me during my divorce. I also see a mother who had her own hurts and disappointments, and in spite of her own challenges, loved, supported and encouraged me. For this I am grateful.

I get to watch my mother be a grandmother and be filled with joy when her grandchildren go running to her. I am blessed to understand how happy she is for their love. I am grateful I got to be my grandmother's favorite grandchild and to experience her love and grace. I am most grateful to be a grandmother who gets to stand on the shoulders of these two women and to pass on my love to my granddaughter.

Being grateful allows me to have what I am grateful for and to experience my mother with love because I am grateful for her love.

When I look back over the events of my life I am grateful for all the low points because I have perspective and I can see how far I have come. Embracing divorce, being molested, intimate partner abuse and all the tragedies of life, defuses their sting and weakens their grip, it makes being happy so much sweeter because I have the bitter experience of being devastated, overwhelmed and depressed.

Gratitude also helps me to clear the way for what I want to create in my life and being grateful in advance helps me to move forward to the life I create. Gratefulness in advance creates positive action and excitement for what is to come. So, be grateful.

Gratitude Journal

A fun way to help move yourself forward and embrace the new life you are creating is through a gratitude journal. A gratitude journal helps you to focus your attention on the positive things in your life and to be thankful for what you create. All you need is notebook, journal or diary to get started. Commit to writing in your journal daily and record at least five thing you are thankful for each day. Include your gratitude for what you are creating.

Examples:

I am thankful and grateful for my family.

I am thankful and grateful for the new job that meets all of my needs.

I am thankful and grateful for global travel that brings me adventure, fun and joy.

Chapter 10

Lean into Love

"Where there is love there is life." — *Mahatma Gandhi*

You are comprised of the good parts, the not so good parts, and the joys and the sorrows from your past and present selves. The tragedies of our lives have helped to shape us just as much as the accomplishments and the joys. Our job is to love every part of who we are and every part of who we are not.

When we are aware of the hurt we cause ourselves and others, we have the power to stop. We have the power to turn away from making ourselves wrong and making ourselves less than who we really are. We get to let go of shame, blame and guilt and we get to lean into love. We have the power to love ourselves and go easy on ourselves. It is time to go easy on ourselves and embrace our humanity, accept the ups and downs of life as just part of being human.

So what you didn't make the basketball team when you were in the 7th grade, let it go. So what you mother abandoned you when you were a baby, let it go. So what you thought your parents loved your sister more than you, let it go. Whatever your complaint is and whatever your struggle, it is all part of being human and guess what, none of us gets to escape this life without the feelings of hurt, disappointments, regret and the fear that comes with being human. So, go easy on yourself, stop beating yourself up for what don't have or didn't do. Stop blaming other people for what went wrong or what could have been. Let all of that go, take responsibility for your life and step into your power. Start leaning into the love you are right now by creating loving actions and a loving environment that confirms the love you feel for you.

Stop putting unsupported meanings on things that happened and did not happen. Just because your partner left you doesn't mean that you are unlovable, it only means he/she left, so let it go. I doesn't mean you are worthless because you were fired from your job; let it go. These are common situations and the meanings given to these situations, it doesn't make it so. Decide right now who you are and how you will let go of meanings that do not serve you.

The life you will love is on the other side of shame, pain, regret and fear. Lean into love, let go of shame, let go of the pain, let go of the regret and let go of the fear, and live your dream life. You can have, do and be whatever you choose.

As for me, I choose joy, I choose peace, I choose acceptance, I choose abundance and I choose love. Lean into love. Be love.

Fontella Moody

Made in the USA
San Bernardino, CA
13 February 2017